THE JOKE BOOK

by

Ena Jam

Illustrated by
Alan Rowe

KNIGHT BOOKS
Hodder and Stoughton

Contents

Introduction	5
Raspberry Ripples	7
Getting the Pip	30
Caught Red-Handed	58
Fruit Basket	72
Blowing Raspberries	87
Raspberries and Cream	114

Text copyright © Ena Jam 1991

Illustrations copyright © Alan Rowe 1991

First published in Great Britain in 1991 by Knight Books

British Library C.I.P.

Cataloguing in Publication Data is available from the British Library

ISBN 0-340-55882-2

The rights of Ena Jam to be identified as the author of the text of this work and of Alan Rowe to be identified as the illustrator of this work has been asserted by them in accordance with the Copyright, Designs and Patents Act 1988.

This book is sold subject to the condition that it shall not, by way of trade or otherwise, be lent, re-sold, hired out or otherwise circulated without the publisher's prior consent in any form of binding or cover other than that in which it is published and without a similar condition including this condition being imposed on the subsequent purchaser.

No part of this publication may be reproduced or transmitted in any form or by any means, electronic or mechanical, including photocopying, recording or any information storage or retrieval system, without either the prior permission in writing from the publisher or a licence, permitting restricted copying. In the United Kingdom such licences are issued by the Copyright Licensing Agency, 90 Tottenham Court Road, London W1P 9HE.

Printed and bound in Great Britain for Hodder and Stoughton Children's Books, a division of Hodder and Stoughton Ltd, Mill Road, Dunton Green, Sevenoaks, Kent TN13 2YA (Editorial Office: 47 Bedford Square, London WC1B 3DP) by Cox & Wyman Ltd., Reading, Berks. Photoset by Rowland Phototypesetting Ltd, Bury St Edmunds, Suffolk.

Introduction

Why a raspberry joke book? What's funny about raspberries, you may ask? They're just summer fruits that are wonderful to eat. True. But it's odd that a word which means a delicious fruit also means an expression of dislike. We all know about blowing raspberries – putting our tongues between almost closed lips and blowing out air to make a rude noise. And we all agree that blowing raspberries *is* funny.

You'll soon discover, as you read this book, that jokes about the other kind of raspberry are very funny, too. Both kinds appear in this book. Blowing Raspberries and Getting the Pip contain jokes about the insulting kind of raspberry; Raspberries and Cream and Raspberry Ripples are full of jokes about the fruity kind. Raspberries are a rich red colour, and so, just for good measure, there is a section of jokes on all other things red, called Caught Red-Handed, as well as one on other fruits, called Fruit Basket. You'll find that reading all the jokes is almost as good fun as sitting down to brimming bowls of the real thing!

Raspberry Ripples

What's red and very noisy?
A raspberry with a drum kit.

What do you get if you cross a raspberry ripple with an elephant?
An ice-cream that never forgets.

What's red, squashy and goes round and round?
A raspberry in a washing-machine.

What's red and goes click, click?
A ballpoint raspberry.

What's red and good at sums?
A raspberry with a calculator.

What was the raspberry doing in the strawberry bed?
It thought strawberries had more fun.

What's red and sweet and always points north?
A magnetic raspberry.

What's red and sweet and wears contact lenses?
A raspberry with poor eyesight.

What happens to endangered raspberries?
They get put in preserves.

DAN: I'll bet I can get you to forget about raspberries.
ANNE: Which raspberries?
DAN: See, you've forgotten already.

Knock, knock.
Who's there?
Bruce.
Bruce who?
Raspberries bruce very easily.

Knock, knock.
Who's there?
Esau.
Esau who?
Esau me picking his raspberries, so let me in quick.

What's red on the inside, grey on the outside, and has long, sticking-out pips?
A raspberry disguised as an elephant.

How does a raspberry feel in December?
Cold.

Knock, knock.
Who's there?
Carrie.
Carrie who?
Carrie these baskets of raspberries for me, I'm tired.

What goes out red and comes in white?
A raspberry in a snowstorm.

What do you call a raspberry with a machine-gun?
'Sir.'

What canes do schoolboys not dislike?
Raspberry canes.

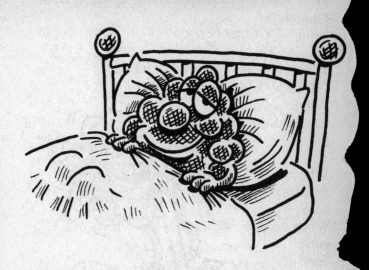

How can you tell raspberries are lazy?
Because they spend all their time in beds.

What do you call a raspberry that drowns in a bowl of double cream?
A non-slimmer.

Knock, knock.
Who's there?
Ros.
Ros who?
Rosberry ripple.

If a raspberry crosses the road, rolls in the dust, then crosses back again, what is it?
A dirty double-crosser.

What's red and squashy and goes slam, slam, slam, slam?
A four-door raspberry.

What's red, squashy and bounces?
A raspberry on a pogo stick.

Why are raspberries safe from pickpockets?
They don't have pockets.

What's the difference between a raspberry and a grapefruit?
A raspberry is red.

How did the mother raspberry spoil her baby?
She left him in the sun too long.

What goes out red and comes in blue?
A raspberry on a cold day.

Knock, knock.
Who's there?
Cassette.
Cassette who?
Cassette your raspberries, I'm afraid.

What's green and squashy and bobs up and down?
A seasick raspberry.

Why do elephants paint their toenails red?
So they can hide in raspberry canes without being seen.

What's red and squashy and travels in a flying saucer?
A Martian raspberry.

What's red and squashy and goes up and down ten times in a row?
A raspberry doing press-ups.

What's red on the inside and green and hairy on the outside?
A raspberry disguised as a gooseberry.

What's red and squashy and never needs ironing?
A drip-dry raspberry.

Knock, knock.
Who's there?
Wayne.
Wayne who?
Wayne are you going to make some more raspberry ice-cream?

What's it called when a raspberry hits a strawberry?
A fruit punch.

What's a raspberry that's two years old?
Bad.

How do you disguise a raspberry?
Give it a false beard and sunglasses.

What's red, wears its knickers over its tights, and fights injustice?
Superaspberry.

Knock, knock.
Who's there?
Farmer.
Farmer who?
Farmer birthday party I'm having a raspberry trifle.

How do you make a raspberry laugh?
Tell it a banana joke.

What's huge, red, and says, 'Fee, fi, fo, fum'?
A giant raspberry.

What's red, squashy and peeling?
A sunburnt raspberry.

What's red, squashy and has sixteen wheels?
A raspberry on roller-skates.

BEN: What's the difference between raspberries and snew?
KEN: What's snew?
BEN: Nothing much. What's new with you?

What do you do with green raspberries?
Send them to school.

What's red, squashy and sneezes a lot?
A raspberry with hay fever.

Knock, knock.
Who's there?
Howard.
Howard who?
Howard the ground is when you slip on some raspberries.

What happened to the little boy who tried to juggle with raspberries?
He got in a jam.

What did the raspberry say to the hungry worm?
'You're boring me.'

What happened when the raspberry fought a hedgehog?
The hedgehog won on points.

JILL: Do you really love me?
JACK: Oh yes.
JILL: Then whisper something soft and sweet in my ear.
JACK: Raspberry meringue.

What's the difference between an apple and a raspberry?
You can't make an apple pie with raspberries.

What's the difference between an elephant and a raspberry?
Elephants don't grow on canes.

Why don't raspberries have bunions?
Because they don't have any feet.

What's red, squashy, and travels through the air at 100 mph?
A flying raspberry.

What's red, squashy and found at the North Pole?
A frozen raspberry.

What did the raspberry say to the greenfly?
'Go away, you're bugging me.'

Why isn't a raspberry green and hairy?
Because if it were it would be a gooseberry.

Why don't raspberries have dandruff?
They haven't any hair.

Knock, knock.
Who's there?
Hanover.
Hanover who?
Hanover the raspberries.

What's the first thing a raspberry does in the morning?
Gets up.

Why don't raspberries ride bicycles?
Because they can't reach the handlebars.

CUSTOMER IN GARDEN CENTRE: Are these raspberries quick growing?
ASSISTANT: They certainly are. Once they're planted you have to stand aside!

JOHN: I've got to write an essay on raspberries.
JIM: You'll have to write very small.

Knock, knock.
Who's there?
Noah.
Noah who?
Noah good place to pick raspberries.

In the high street was a shop that sold fruit and fish. Late one afternoon a man walked in and asked for two large trout.

'I'm sorry, sir,' said the assistant, 'but we have no trout left. We've sold out of all our fish today. In fact, we've sold out of nearly all our fruit, too. All I have left are two punnets of raspberries. Would you like those?'

'Don't be silly,' replied the man. 'How can I go home and tell my wife I've caught half a kilo of raspberries?'

Why was the little raspberry worried?
Because all his friends were in a jam.

TEACHER: If raspberries were eighty pence a kilo, how many kilos would you get for two pounds forty?
SANDY: None.
TEACHER: None?
SANDY: No. If I had two pounds forty I'd go to the cinema.

TEACHER: When the animals went into the Ark, they went in pairs.
SILLY SUE: Worms didn't, Miss, they went in raspberries.

Why do raspberry growers hate weeds?
Because if you give them an inch they'll take a yard.

What's red, squashy, and drinks from the wrong side of the glass?
A raspberry with hiccups.

Knock, knock.
Who's there?
Thumping.
Thumping who?
Thumping green and slimy is climbing out of your raspberries!

What's the best way to raise raspberries?
With a spoon.

What did the raspberry say to the strawberry?
Nothing, raspberries can't talk.

GILL: Guess what I've got in my hands?
BILL: A raspberry playing the piano.
GILL: Oh, you peeped!

VISITOR TO CHILD IN GARDEN: Is your mother in?
CHILD: Well, I'm not weeding the raspberry canes because I want to!

Why are raspberry seeds like gateposts?
Because they propagate.

Why is a Boy Scout like a tin of raspberries?
They're both prepared.

What's red and flickers?
A raspberry with a loose connection.

What's red and plays music?
A transistor raspberry.

How many raspberries can you get into an empty two-litre basin?
Only one. After that it isn't empty any more.

Knock, knock.
Who's there?
Handsome.
Handsome who?
Handsome raspberries through the window and I'll clear off.

MRS FIMBLE: I sent my son round to you an hour ago for a kilo of raspberries and you've only sent me half. Is there something wrong with your scales?
GREENGROCER: There's nothing wrong with our scales, madam. Have you tried weighing your son?

One winter morning a sparrow was watching a snail climbing up a raspberry cane. 'Why are you doing that?' asked the sparrow. 'There aren't any raspberries on it!'

'There will be by the time I get up there,' replied the snail.

TEACHER: I saw you stealing a punnet of raspberries from outside the greengrocer's yesterday, but I was pleased to see that you put it back. You realised that you were doing wrong.
NAUGHTY NORA: No, Miss, it had maggots in it.

What's the difference between a raspberry and a jumbo jet?
A raspberry can't fly the Atlantic without refuelling.

What's long, red and shoots grouse?
A double-barrelled raspberry.

What's red and gargles?
A raspberry with a sore throat.

What's the difference between a raspberry and an elephant?
A raspberry always forgets.

What's red and travels underwater?
A raspberry in a submarine.

Why is someone learning to sing like someone opening a tin of raspberries?
They both have trouble with the key.

When do raspberries paint themselves purple?
When they want to hide in a bramble bush.

What's red and sweet and croaks?
A raspberry with laryngitis.

How do you tell a raspberry from a lemon?
If it's red, it's probably a raspberry.

Knock, knock.
Who's there?
Bernardette.
Bernardette who?
Bernardette all of my raspberries.

DENNIS: Mum, these raspberries are hard.
MUM, TAKING A SPOONFUL AND TRYING THEM: They seem soft enough to me.
DENNIS: Those are the ones I've been chewing for the last fifteen minutes.

What magazine do raspberry growers read?
The Weeder's Digest.

What's red and shoots off canes at 100 mph?
A jet-propelled raspberry.

Getting The Pip

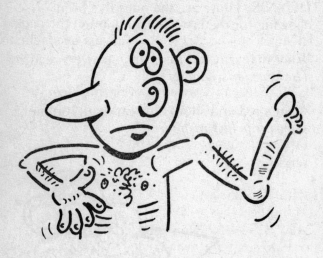

DAVE: What I always say about Tom is that he's a man of many parts.
MAVE: Yes, but their assembly leaves a lot to be desired.

KAREN: Your brother is out of this world!
SHARON: I often wish he were!

'The trouble with Harold is that he wants everyone to worship the ground he crawled out of.'

'Gloria's the sort of girl who only cares for a man's company if he owns it.'

POLLY: When our ex-headmistress died they buried her face down.
MOLLY: Why was that?
POLLY: So she could see where she was going.

JIM: Our biology teacher's a pain in the neck.
KIM: I'll say he is. He could give a headache to an aspirin.

'George has an answer to every problem. Trouble is, it's usually the wrong one!'

'Brian is a man with polish.'
'But only on his shoes!'

MRS JONES: I hear Mrs Dean is very economical.
MRS BROWN: Well, she certainly seems to save on soap and water.

LYNNE: I don't think I look too good in a sweater.
FLYNN: No, the wool looked better on the sheep.

'Charles hasn't been himself recently.'
'I thought I'd noticed an improvement!'

LARRY: What do you mean, Yuletide greetings?
BARRY: Lend me twenty pounds and you'll tide me over 'til Christmas.

Jim was showing his holiday pictures to his school friends. One photo showed him riding a donkey on the beach.

'That's a good picture of you,' said his friend Bill. 'But who's that sitting on your back?'

BAZ: Sarah loves Nature.
CHAS: That's very good of her considering what Nature did to her!

MUM: Why don't you go out and play? Gandpa's in the garden, you could play Cowboys and Indians with him.
DENNIS: No we couldn't, Mum.
MUM: Why not?
DENNIS: 'Cos he's been scalped already.

'Mike has a leaning towards tall, well-built blondes.'
'Yes, but they always push him back!'

'Harold's a bit dull until you know him, and when you do he's a real bore!'

'Emily eats like a bird.'
'Yes, a starving vulture!'

'Tim's lucky in one way. If he went out of his mind, no one would notice the difference.'

BEN: My sister says she'll only marry someone who can take a joke.
KEN: That's the only kind who'd take her!

'Alan's always changing his mind.'
'Mmm. Pity he doesn't change his clothes more often.'

SUE: I've changed my mind.
PRUE: Does the new one work any better?

MILLY: Why do you say your Dad is good for people's health?
BILLY: When they see him coming they go for a long walk.

'Sheila's not that bad looking. She's only got one blemish between her ears.'
'Yes, her face!'

GLENDA: Darren's girl crazy.
BRENDA: Yes, they won't go out with him, that's why he's crazy.

JERRY: Bertie was a war baby.
TERRY: I expect his parents started fighting after they'd first seen him.

JACK: Mum's watching her weight.
JILL: Yes, watching it go up!

'Bill's so fat he can take a shower without getting his feet wet!'
'And Ben's so fat he can sit round the table all by himself!'

MR LARGE: I don't know what happens to all the grocery money.
MRS LARGE: Stand sideways and look at yourself in the mirror and you'll see!

'People like Keith don't grow on trees – they swing from them.'

'When Stuart goes to the zoo he has to buy two tickets – one to get in and the other to get out.'

ADAM: Your brother's not very popular at school, is he?
ANGIE: No. If he ever needs a friend I reckon he'll have to buy a dog.

KATE: Your sister's such a nice girl. Everybody likes her.
KEVIN: Yeah, 20,000 flies can't be wrong!

CYNTHIA: The stork brought my new baby sister.
SAMANTHA: Did it drop her from a great height?

MRS FRUMP: Whenever I'm down in the dumps I buy myself a new pair of shoes.
MRS FRIMP: Oh, so that's where you get them, is it?

'They make a perfect couple, don't they?'
'Yes. He's a pill and she's a headache.'

MRS GREEN: I hear she serves health food.
MRS BROWN: Yes, if you're not in good health you don't survive it.

JANE: John only goes out at Hallowe'en.
WAYNE: Why?
JANE: It's the only time he's seen as normal.

'I never act stupid.'
'No, with you it's the real thing.'

'Graham's so dirty his mother washes him with oven cleaner.'

SALLY: When Dave had his photo taken the photographer wouldn't develop it.
WALLY: Why not?
SALLY: I think he was afraid of being alone in a dark-room with it.

'Elizabeth looks much prettier when I'm not wearing glasses.'

'Last time I saw a face like Cyril's it had a fish hook in it.'

WILLIE: James was at college for ten years. He's a DD.
MILLY: A Doctor of Divinity?
WILLIE: No, a dum-dum.

'You can tell she's a classical scholar. Her kitchen shows she's an expert on ancient grease.'

'He's going out of his mind. And his mind's glad he's leaving.'

'The children at Emma's school are so tough the teachers play truant.'

'Simon has a very sympathetic face.'
'Yes, it provokes everyone's sympathy.'

'Maureen never says an unkind word about anyone.'
'That's because she only talks about herself.'

'Trouble is, she talks like a photocopier.'
'A photocopier?'
'Yes, she keeps repeating herself.'

ANNE: Betty had a coming-out party.
DAN: I bet they took one look at her and sent her back in again.

'Waiter, if this is coffee, bring me tea. If this is tea, bring me coffee.'

'When my husband went to the doctor about his poor memory they made him pay in advance!'

BERT: Karen works effortlessly.
GERT: Yes. She never lifts a finger.

CLARA: What do you mean, 'plan ahead'?
SARAH: Look in the mirror. If you'd already done so, you'd be better looking!

MRS GRUMBLE: I wish I had my husband back.
MRS CRUMBLE: Where is he?
MRS GRUMBLE: I swapped him for a computer.
MRS CRUMBLE: And now you miss him?
MRS GRUMBLE: No, now I want a fax machine.

'Peter must have a sixth sense, because he shows no sign of the other five.'

NORA: He's got lovely blue eyes.
DORA: If he's not careful he'll have two black ones.

ELLIE: Nick's a real pain in the neck.
NELLIE: It could be worse. He could have a twin brother.

'Doreen sings like a pirate.'
'What do you mean?'
'Murder on the high Cs.'

MRS MOUSETROUSER: Who's that lady with the little wart?
MRS STOATSKIRT: Shh, that's her husband.

'Do you think he looks bad?'
'He could look worse, if I had better eyesight.'

TED: My sister's on a crash diet.
RED: I thought she looked a bit of a wreck.

MUM: Why did you paint your teacher in oils?
MIKE: Because she looks like a sardine.

MRS SNOOTY: My daughter plays the piano. She's had many requests.
MRS BOOTY: So I've heard – but she still keeps on playing.

'He thinks he's elevated above all others.'
'He should be, by the neck!'

'He's so mean that if he were a ghost he wouldn't even give you a fright.'

AUNTIE: Are you a good boy, Alec?
ALEC: No, I'm the kind my mother doesn't like me to play with.

'You remind me of raspberry trifle.'
'Why, because I'm so sweet?'
'No, because you make me sick.'

'He's got the kind of face you don't want to remember but can't forget.'

LAURA: He's a sleepwalking idiot, but he cured himself.
DORA: How?
LAURA: He took his bus fare to bed with him every night.

'Why did your brother go to the dentist?'
'To have a wisdom tooth put in.'

CHRISSIE: I'm thinking hard.
CISSIE: You mean it's hard for you to think?

ANDY: If you saw me standing beside a monster, what fruit would it remind you of?
MANDY: A pear.

Where do bad choirboys get sent?
Singapore.

MAVE: You'd make a wonderful dancer except for two things.
DAVE: What?
MAVE: Your feet.

HARRY: That's Cecilia. Her mother almost lost her when she was young.
LARRY: Perhaps she didn't take her far enough into the woods?

CLARA: He's so daft he videos TV programmes he doesn't want to watch.
SARAH: What does he do with them?
CLARA: He plays them when he's out.

'The trouble with that movie was that they shot too much film and not enough actors.'

JENNY: When I die I'm going to leave my brain to science.
LENNY: I suppose every little helps.

PATIENT: I feel like my old self again.
DOCTOR: In that case, you need more treatment.

HATTIE: Why did your brother have to leave the navy?
MATTIE: They transferred him to submarines.
HATTIE: Why did that mean he had to leave?
MATTIE: Because he always slept with the windows open.

'He's so daft that when he went hitch-hiking he got up early to avoid the traffic.'

'Lettie talks so much that when she goes on holiday she has to put suntan lotion on her tongue.'

'He's like blotting paper. He takes it all in, but he gets it all backwards.'

DEAN: You shouldn't have trodden on that spider, they're lucky.
JEAN: This one wasn't.

'Did you hear about the dumbo on the oil rig?'
'He was so stupid that when a helicopter flew over he threw bread to feed it.'

HIL: I went to the zoo last weekend.
BILL: I was there too.
HIL: Funny, I looked in all the cages but I didn't see you.

FRED: How long can someone live without a brain?
NED: I don't know. How old are you?

BRYN: How dare you call me deaf and dumb!
GWYN: I never said you were deaf.

MICK: Paul's really fat, isn't he?
DICK: He certainly is. He had mumps for a week before anyone realised.

ALBERT: Alice's house is very small, isn't it?
ALFRED: I'll say! Even the mice have round shoulders.

TEACHER: See if you can put this sentence another way. 'He was bent on seeing her.'
JACK: The sight of her doubled him up.
TEACHER: No, not quite, Jack. Try again with another sentence. 'Her beauty was timeless.'
JACK: Her face would stop a clock.

BETTY: There's only one way of making money honestly.
HETTIE: How's that?
BETTY: Trust you not to know it!

GILL: I thought you were going to marry Bill? You said it was love at first sight.
GINA: It was the second and third sights that put me off.

JOHNNY: Did I tell you the new joke I heard yesterday?
DONNY: Is it funny?
JOHNNY: Yes.
DONNY: Then you didn't.

GLORIA: Do you think I'll lose my looks as I get older?
GLENDA: With luck, yes.

'He's a very boring man, but he does have occasional flashes of silence.'

ELSIE: She looks like Helen Black.
EDNA: You should see her in red.

FRAN: What's the difference between a sigh, a Rolls Royce, and a jackass?
DAN: I don't know.
FRAN: A sigh is 'oh dear', a Rolls Royce is too dear . . .
DAN: And what's a jackass?
FRAN: You, dear!

LUCY: Can you lend me ten pence? I want to phone a friend.
LENNIE: Here's twenty pence. Phone all your friends.

CYRIL: Mum! All the kids at school call me Bighead!
MUM: Never mind, dear. Just run round to the greengrocer's and bring me three kilos of potatoes in your cap.

BOB: Did you hear my last joke?
ROB: I certainly hope so.

PATTIE: Don't scratch your head.
HATTIE: Why not?
PATTIE: You'll get splinters in your fingers.

MO: The trouble with Gilbert is that he's like a summer cold.
JOE: How's that?
MO: You can't get rid of him.

MR FAT: You look as though you've lived through a famine.
MR THIN: And you look as if you've caused one.

MRS CRUMP: My husband always carries a photograph of me over his heart. It once saved his life when someone tried to shoot him.
MRS CRIMP: I'm not surprised. Your face would stop anything.

'I hear she always has to have the last word.'
'It wouldn't be so bad if she ever reached it.'

DILLY: I'll have you know I have the face of a sixteen-year-old.
BILLY: Well you'd better give it back, you're getting it all wrinkled.

MR JONES: When I die I want to be buried at sea.
MR SMITH: Why?
MR JONES: Because my wife says she wants to dance on my grave.

BARBER: How do you want your hair cut, sonny?
LITTLE BOY: Like Dad's, with a hole in the middle.

MRS POORCOOK: There's a man downstairs eating my home-made rhubarb pie!
MR POORCOOK: Shall I call the police or an ambulance?

MRS NEWLYWED: Darling, we've been married twelve whole months!
MR NEWLYWED: Feels more like a year to me.

MRS LONGWED: I've given you the best years of my life.
MR LONGWED: Do you want a receipt?

MRS LONGSUFFERING: One more word out of you and I go back to mother!
MR LONGSUFFERING: Taxi!

'His wife worships him, doesn't she?'
'She must do. He says she puts burnt offerings in front of him three times a day.'

'He was so embarrassed when he was asked to take off his mask at the fancy dress party.'
'Why?'
'He wasn't wearing one.'

'His right eye must be really interesting.'
'Why do you say that?'
'Because his left eye looks at it all the time.'

'Looks aren't everything.'
'In his case, they aren't anything.'

ALEC: Dick's so dumb he thinks a football coach has four wheels.
ALAN: Well how many does it have?

GARY: Are you trying to make a fool out of me?
MARY: No. I never interfere with Nature.

HARRY: I live on garlic alone.
LARRY: I'm not surprised. Anyone who lives on garlic can't help but live alone.

TRACY: Your husband seems to be a man of rare gifts.
STACEY: Yes – it's been years since he gave me a present.

MRS DIM: I hear your son is in the school football team. What position does he play?
MRS DUMN: I think he's one of the drawbacks.

CAROL: Did you say he spreads happiness wherever he goes?
DARRYL: No, I said *whenever* he goes.

TONY: Did you hear about the fool who only says 'No'?
RONY: No.
TONY: Oh, so it's you, is it?

JILL: Now we're engaged I hope you'll give me a ring.
JACK: Of course! What's your phone number?

SHANE: Everyone in my block asks my advice and follows it.
WAYNE: I believe you. You're a natural blockhead.

PHIL: I'm burning with love for you.
GILL: Oh don't make a fuel of yourself.

GILES: I didn't come here to be insulted!
MILES: Oh really? Where do you usually go?

TOMMY: Why do you call your granny Treasure?
TRACY: Because I wonder where she was dug up.

SIMON: *Je t'adore.*
SUSIE: Shut it yourself!

KAREN: Do you love me?
DARREN: Yes. I'd die for you.
KAREN: You're always saying that, but you never do it.

Caught Red Handed

Why did the fireman have red braces?
Because he was a sloppy tomato soup eater.

What's red and goes putt, putt, putt?
An outboard apple.

What's big and red and hides its face?
An embarrassed elephant.

What's red, covered in pips and lights up?
An electric strawberry.

Did you hear the sad tale of the two blood cells?
They loved in vein.

They say blood's thicker than water.
So what – so's custard!

HENRY: I hear you have a bloodhound.
HERBERT: Yes, but he's not much use.
HENRY: Why's that?
HERBERT: Yesterday he bit my finger, saw the blood and fainted.

What's big, red, and lies upside-down at the side of the road?
A dead bus.

What ribbon do lawyers use?
Red tape.

What happens to people who wear rose-coloured spectacles?
They end up seeing red.

BOB: Why's your jacket on fire?
ROB: Because it's a blazer.

TEACHER: Give me a definition of the word 'information'.
PUPIL: It's how the Red Arrows fly.

What's blue, V-shaped and flies?
The Red Arrows in disguise.

Why did the beach blush?
Because the seaweed.

TEACHER: If you bought twenty-five jam tarts for seventy-five pence what would each one be?
BRIGHT BILLY: Stale.

MRS RUMPEL: What do you think about Red China?
MRS FRUMPEL: It depends what food you serve on it.

MARJORIE: Why do children from your school wear red?
MAUREEN: To warn people that they're dangerous.

Did you hear about the two lorries on the M1? One had a cargo of red paint, and one had a cargo of purple paint, and they crashed at a junction. The drivers were marooned.

PAT: What's your favourite colour?
WAT: Red.
PAT: And what's your favourite animal?
WAT: A horse.
PAT: And what's your favourite number?
WAT: Ten.
PAT: When did you last see a red horse with ten legs?

What bird is red and a criminal?
A robin.

What's big, red and eats rocks?
A big, red, rock-eater.

What's black when you get it, red when you use it, and grey when you've finished with it?
Coal.

MUM: Why is your face so red?
JIMMY: I ran up the road to stop a fight.
MUM: That was very good of you. Who was fighting?
JIMMY: Me and another boy.

Why did the windowpane blush?
Because it saw the weatherstrip.

How do you part the Red Sea?
With a sea-saw.

Who invented the fireplace?
Alfred the Grate.

How does a fireplace feel when it's full of fuel?
Grate-ful.

Who invented fire?
A bright spark.

What lives if you feed it but dies if you water it?
A fire.

MARY: My Mum had a blazing fire in the kitchen yesterday.
GARY: That's nice.
MARY: Not really. We don't have a fireplace.

Who's assured of a warm welcome wherever he goes?
A fireman.

BILL: This match won't light.
GILL: Funny, it did this morning.

Why do traffic lights turn red?
You'd turn red if you had to stop and go in the middle of the road.

CUSTOMER: Have you a dress to match my eyes?
SHOP ASSISTANT: Sorry, we don't sell bloodshot dresses.

What do you call a Russian fish in a detective story?
A red herring.

If a red house is built of red bricks, and a yellow house is built of yellow bricks, what's a greenhouse made of?
Glass.

What's red and dangerous?
Shark-infested raspberries.

BEN: Why are you all covered in cuts and bruises?
KEN: I went on a school trip.

BIOLOGY TEACHER: There are thousands of kilometres of blood vessels in the body.
SHEILA: No wonder my blood's tired.

What are blue-blooded and go 'woof'?
The Queen's corgis.

There once was a young man from Derry
Who ran in the races at Kerry.
On the 29th lap
His braces went snap
And his face went as red as a cherry.

Why does a man wear red, white and blue braces?
To hold up his red, white and blue trousers.

Two American tourists were on holiday in Russia, and were being shown round Moscow by their guide, Rudolf. When they were being shown round the Kremlin one of the Americans said, 'It's snowing outside.'

Rudolf corrected him. 'No, sir, it is raining,' he said.

The American persisted. 'I'm sure it's snow,' he said.

His wife interrupted. 'Rudolf the Red knows rain, dear,' she said.

What's black and white and red all over?
An embarrassed penguin.

A man went to a kennels to buy a dog.

'Would you like a red setter?' asked the attendant.

'No, not a red setter.'

'Then how about a golden labrador?'

'No, not a golden labrador. What I want is a black and white dog.'

'Why do you want a black and white dog?' asked the attendant.

'Because the licence is cheaper,' replied the man.

What do vampires go sailing in?
Blood vessels.

Where did Dracula keep his money?
In a blood bank.

Mr Wimp had parked his white car outside the pub while he had a drink with a friend. When he left the pub, he discovered that someone had painted half his car bright red.

In great rage, he went back into the pub and demanded, 'Who painted my car red?'

A huge, 140-kilo man got up and walked slowly over. 'I did,' he said. 'What of it?'

'Er, I just wondered when you were going to paint the other side,' stammered Mr Wimp.

LOST: School scarf by boy with red and white stripes.

Why did the lobster blush?
Because it saw the salad dressing.

LADY CUSTOMER: Can I try on that red dress in the window?
SHOP ASSISTANT: You'll have to use the changing-room like everyone else, I'm afraid.

BARBER: When you came in were you wearing a red scarf?
CUSTOMER: No.
BARBER: Oh dear, I must have cut your throat.

'Vicar! Come quickly! The church is on fire!'
'Holy smoke!'

What happened when the red sauce chased the brown sauce?
It couldn't ketchup.

There were two tomatoes on a plate. Which one was the cowboy?
Neither, they were both redskins.

The big red bus was very full, and a man trying to get on it was pushed off by the people inside.
'There's no room,' they said. 'It's full up!'
  'But you must let me on,' pleaded the man.
  'What's so special about you?' they asked.
  'I'm the driver,' he replied.

What does a white sheep become if it jumps in the Red Sea?
Wet.

MR GREEN: Why is your car red on one side and blue on the other?
MR BROWN: So that if I have an accident the witnesses will contradict one another!

MUM: What did you learn at school today?
PAT: How to leave early by putting red ink up my nose.

LIL: What's got red and yellow stripes, a hairy body and six legs?
WILL: I don't know. Why do you ask?
LIL: Because one just crawled up your trouser leg.

Did you hear about the man who was suspected of stealing twenty-five kilos of strawberries from a 'pick your own' fruit farm?
He was caught red-handed.

'Doctor, Doctor, I think I've got measles.'
'That's a rash statement.'

Fruit Basket

What's yellow, curved and covered in red spots?
A banana with measles.

What's brown, wrinkled and drinks from the wrong side of the glass?
A prune with hiccups.

MUM: When Mrs Cushion gave you an apple, what did you say?
SUSIE: Will you peel it, please?

Knock, knock.
Who's there?
Garter.
Garter who?
I've garter loverly bunch of coconuts.

Why did the peach stop rolling down the hill?
It ran out of juice.

What happened to the man who stole ten kilos of rhubarb?
He was put into custardy.

JOHN: Does an apple a day keep the doctor away?
MUM: Yes.
JOHN: Then give me one quickly – I've just shot my catapult through his window.

DAD: Why do you call your teacher Peach?
DAVE: Because she's got a heart of stone.

What's a melancholy?
A sheepdog that likes eating melons.

Knock, knock.
Who's there?
Anne.
Anne who?
Anne apple just fell on my head.

'Doctor, Doctor, I've just eaten an apple, an apricot, a banana, six dates, ten figs, one melon, a pear, a bowl of raspberries and a bowl of strawberries, and I've got a stomach ache.'
   'How interesting! Do you always eat your fruit in alphabetical order?'

What's purple and crazy?
A grape nut.

What's a fresh fruit?
One that makes cheeky remarks to a gardener.

What kind of apple is bad-tempered?
A crab-apple.

Why are roller-skates like banana skins?
Both are responsible for the fall of man.

TEACHER: If you had seven apples in a bag and your friend took four, what would you have?
SIMON: A fight, Miss.

NICK: Watch out for worms when you're eating those blackberries.
MICK: When I eat these blackberries, the worms had better watch out for themselves.

TEACHER: What's a prickly pear?
SALLY: Er, two hedgehogs, Miss.

What's the difference between rhubarb and custard and rhubarb and cement?
Not a lot in some places!

A man met an old friend he hadn't seen for many years. 'I hear your first two wives died after eating poisoned fruit, and the third has just fallen out of a window. It's a bit odd, isn't it?' he asked.
    'Not at all,' replied his former friend. 'She wouldn't eat the poisoned fruit.'

Knock, knock.
Who's there?
Carmen.
Carmen who?
Carmen get your fruit.

What's a good way to put on weight?
Eat a peach, swallow the centre and you've gained a stone.

What's squashy, green and in the North Sea?
Grape Britain.

How can you tell the time with a fruit?
Eat a strawberry and count the pips.

How do bad cooks make baked apples?
By setting orchards on fire.

HARRY: I thought there was a choice of fresh fruit for pudding?
DINNER LADY: There is. Take it or leave it.

A silly old lady from Hyde
Ate so many apples, she died.
The apples fermented
Inside the lamented
Making cider insider 'er inside!

What does a vegetarian fruit earn?
Celery.

MUM: If you eat another strawberry tart you'll burst.
FENTON: Too late, Mum, I've already eaten another one!

What's purple and can be seen from the moon?
The Grape Wall of China.

FREDA: I'm so unlucky my plastic fruit went bad.
FRED: I'm even more unlucky. My stuffed dog ran away.

What would you feel if you ate lunch at a vineyard?
Grapeful!

TEACHER: If I had nine oranges in one hand and seven oranges in the other, what would I have?
SMART SUE: Big hands, Miss.

Where do you learn how to make fruit ice-cream?
At sundae school.

Knock, knock.
Who's there?
Aida.
Aida who?
Aida lotta fruit and now I feela ill.

FARMER: What are you doing in my pear tree?
IAN: One of your pears fell down and I was putting it back.

There was a young lady called Nellie
Who ate lots and lots of fruit jelly,
Then rhubarb and custard,
Bananas and mustard –
Which gave her a pain in her belly.

Knock, knock.
Who's there?
Diana.
Diana who?
Diana thirst, can I have a glass of fruit juice please?

Knock, knock.
Who's there?
Almond.
Almond who?
Almond your side.

What's rhubarb?
Celery with high blood pressure.

DOCTOR: How are you, Mrs Feather?
MRS FEATHER: Well, you know you told me to eat some fruit every night after my bath?
DOCTOR: Yes.
MRS FEATHER: Well, after I've drunk the bath I can't manage the fruit as well.

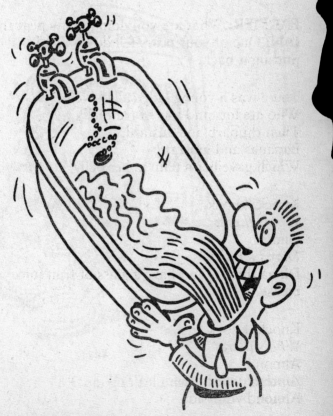

ANNE: There's a lot of juice in this lemon.
DAN: Yes, more than meets the eye.

What can't you do if you put 300 melons in the fridge?
Shut the door.

Which fruit can mend leaking taps?
A plum-ber.

Knock, knock.
Who's there?
Amanda.
Amanda who?
Amanda rin orange.

Did you hear about the woman who went on a bananas and coconut diet?
She didn't lose any weight but she couldn't half climb trees!

MUM: Were you caught eating the apples in Mr Crump's orchard?
CHRIS: Yes.
MUM: How did he punish you?
CHRIS: He didn't. He said I'd been punished enough already. You see, they were cooking apples.

What would happen if the world ran out of olive oil?
You'd get rusty olives.

What's the best time to pick apples?
When the farmer's dog is tied up!

Why did the apple turnover?
Because it saw the banana split.

Knock, knock.
Who's there?
Gorilla.
Gorilla who?
Gorilla n'apple dumpling for me and I'll be right over.

Knock, knock.
Who's there?
General Lee.
General Lee who?
General Lee I like fruit puddings.

A customer rings the greengrocer to complain that she had ordered ten peaches but he had only sent nine.
   'I know,' he said. 'But one was bad, so I threw it away.'

'Doctor, Doctor, I feel like an orange.'
'Have you tried playing squash?'

'Doctor, Doctor, I feel like an apple.'
'We must get to the core of this.'

DEN: Why do you hang garlic on your doors and windows?
BEN: To keep vampires away.
DEN: But there aren't any vampires!
BEN: That just shows how well it works.

Knock, knock.
Who's there?
Harriet.
Harriet who?
Harriet all of my fruit.

What's an oversized pumpkin called?
A plumpkin.

What can a whole peach do that half a peach cannot do?
Look round.

What's a green pickled highwayman called?
Dick Gherkin.

Knock, knock.
Who's there?
Banana.
Banana who?
Banana split so ice-creamed.

'Waiter, there's soap in this fruit salad!'
'That's to wash it down with, sir.'

What nuts can you use to build a house?
Walnuts.

'Waiter, this fruit juice is all cloudy.'
'Don't worry, sir, it's just the glass that is dirty.'

Blowing Raspberries

'He goes to the dentist twice a year – once for each tooth!'

ENA: His skin is so smooth.
SHEENA: Yes, as smooth as a prune's.

'She has a pretty head on her shoulders.'
'Yes, it's a pity she has no neck in between.'

'She's a light eater.'
'Yes, as soon as it's light she starts eating.'

'She's as pretty as a spring flower.'
'Yes, a cauliflower.'

NINA: Why's your sister called Angel?
TINA: Because she's always harping on about things.

LILY: My Dad's a dustman.
MILLY: I thought he had a certain air about him.

DELIA: Our teacher's around forty-five.
CELIA: Yes, he's been around it a few times now.

'When they gave her a facelift the crane broke.'

FRED: Why's he called Caterpillar?
TED: Because he got where he is by crawling.

MARK: He's the big cheese in this office.
CLARK: It looks as if he's going mouldy to me.

PAUL: I need to lose two stones.
SAUL: Why don't you cut off your head?

TESSIE: What does your brother do?
BESSIE: He's at university.
TESSIE: Still? But he's been there ten years!
BESSIE: Yes, he's got more degrees than a thermometer.

'He's so crooked he has to screw his hat on.'

VAL: I wonder what my IQ is.
CAL: Don't. It's nothing.

'He's like a drip – you can hear him but you can't turn him off.'

'He's so old, when he was a boy Billy wasn't even a kid.'

'He can't play the violin – he can't decide which chin to put it under.'

'He's so bald you have to wear sunglasses to look at him on a bright day.'

DAISY: Why do they call her an after-dinner speaker?
MAISIE: Because every time she speaks to a man she's after a dinner.

'He's a man of few words.'
'Trouble is, he keeps repeating them.'

GILL: Does your mother lie about her age?
BILL: Not really. She says she's as old as Dad and then lies about *his* age.

'He started at the bottom and liked it so much he stayed there.'

TEL: Is she really ugly?
DEL: Put it this way, when she walks into a room the budgie stops whistling.

GLEN: What's your brother going to be when he grows up?
BEN: An old-age pensioner.

'You're pretty dirty, Jimmy.'
'I'm even prettier clean.'

'He's someone who's going places.'
'The sooner the better!'

'Why's he called Bead?'
'The girls all string him along.'

BRENDA: That photograph you took of me doesn't do me justice.
BRIAN: You don't want justice, you want mercy.

'I wouldn't say he has a turned-up nose, but every time he sneezes he blows off his cap.'

'He's a chemist's delight – a real pill!'

'He took her for better or worse, but he didn't mean *that* much worse!'

'Anne wanted a man clever enough to make a lot of money – and stupid enough to spend it all on her!'

BOYD: Accept my opinion, for what it's worth.
LLOYD: OK. Here's a penny.

STELLA: I have a perfect shape.
BELLA: Yes. Perfectly round.

'I don't know how you could ever love a man who was stupid enough to have married you!'

EMIL: Look at old baldy over there!
ELMER: That's the first time I've seen a parting with ears!

CHERYL: Her stories always have a happy ending.
BERYL: Everyone's certainly happy when they *have* ended.
CHERYL: Yes, the Noise Abatement Society should send her a button – for her lip!

'Amelia's singing is getting better. Now we only need to put cottonwool in one ear.'

'He's so stupid, when the driving instructor told him to dip his headlights he drove his car into the river.'

MABEL: He can trace his family tree back for generations.
MINNIE: Yes, back to the time his family lived in it.

CAROL: That comedian needs better gags.
DARRYL: Yes, to stop him opening his mouth.

EVE: You can't call Dudley a quitter.
STEVE: Certainly not. He's been sacked from every job he's had.

SUE: Do you like this dress? It's over 50 years old.
PRUE: Did you make it yourself?

JEAN: That ointment the doctor gave me made my skin smart.
DEAN: Better put some on your head, then.

CLARA: I've traced my ancestors back to royalty.
SARAH: King Kong?

WITNESS: He was drunk as a judge.
JUDGE: Don't you mean 'drunk as a lord'?
WITNESS: Yes, my lord.

'How would you have played that shot?' asked the new golfer.
'In disguise!' replied his partner.

DALE: A few minutes with Sally and I feel like jumping for joy.
VALE: I feel like jumping off a cliff.

MRS SHUFFLEBOTTOM: My husband's one in a million.
MRS SIDEBOTTOM: Really? I thought he was won in a raffle.

BOSS: Why are you late this morning?
SECRETARY: I'm afraid I overslept.
BOSS: You mean you sleep at home as well?

MUM: Now you've finished, you can say Grace.
OLLIE: Thanks a bunch for lunch, Lord.
MUM: That wasn't much of a Grace!
OLLIE: It wasn't much of a lunch either.

'He holds people open-mouthed with his stories.'
'That's because they can't stop yawning.'

'His wallet's full of big bills. The gas bill, the phone bill . . .'

KEN: Our history teacher's very old, isn't he?
LEN: Yes. When he was at school, I expect history was called current affairs.

'She married him for what he was – ugly, old, and very, very rich.'

MOLLY: My boss said he was sorry I was leaving next month.
POLLY: He was probably hoping you were leaving this month.

BILLY: My girlfriend's different from other girls.
GILLIE: I'll bet she is. She's the only one who'll go out with you.

The party started at six sharp. And ended at eight dull.

BOSS: Why do you want to take time off next week?
CLERK: To get married, sir.
BOSS: What idiot woman would want to marry you?
CLERK: Your daughter, sir.

'He's so insincere the only genuine thing about him is his false teeth!'

ANNIE: There's no point in telling you a joke with a double meaning.
FANNY: Why not?
ANNIE: You wouldn't get either of them.

'He does lots of exercise.'
'He's certainly long-winded, yes.'

'I don't know what makes you so stupid, but whatever it is, it works.'

DICK: That singer's not very good, is she?
FLICK: No. I reckon if Van Gogh were still alive and heard her he'd cut off *both* his ears.

ED: Cyril has a pigtail.
TED: If you pull it he probably goes 'oink'!

TINA: Harold's one in a million.
NINA: Thank goodness!

MARY: Why does your brother stand on his head?
GARY: He likes turning things over in his mind.

MRS DIMM: I'm afraid my daughter is not very bright. I don't think she'll manage to find a job.
MRS DUMB: She could always be a ventriloquist's dummy.

BONNIE: Two heads are better than one.
DONNIE: In your case, none is better than one.

MO: Percy's face reflects his thoughts.
JOE: Yes, he has a blank expression.

RON: Veronica is not a simple person, she has great depths.
DON: Yes, depths of ignorance.

TODD: Don't you think that comedian is funny?
ROD: No. It's when I listen to him that I realise humour is a serious business.

HORACE: We should take Henry at face value.
HERBERT: With that face, that's not worth much!

'I reckon your mother should have kept the stork and thrown you away.'

'David's so daft he looked at a mirror with his eyes shut to see what he looked like when he was asleep.'

'I wouldn't say he was the world's worst athlete, but if he ran a bath he'd come in second.'

JENNY: Why do you call your boyfriend Caesar?
BENNY: Because he's got a lot of Gaul.

MR SNOOTY: I'm a well-known antiques collector.
MR POOTY: Yes, I've seen your wife.

TILLY: People keep telling me I'm beautiful.
BILLY: Some people have vivid imaginations.

MAY: I wish Tom would stop acting the fool.
FAY: He's not acting.

GIRL IN CINEMA QUEUE: Look at that man over there. Isn't he the ugliest man you've ever seen?
HER NEIGHBOUR: He's my husband.
GIRL: Oh, I'm so sorry.
NEIGHBOUR: *You're* sorry!

TEACHER: I've taught you all I know, and you're still ignorant!

ROSE: I can marry anyone I please, so there!
RICHARD: But you have to find someone you please, my dear!

DARREN: My brother's got a memory like an elephant.
SHARON: And the shape to go with it.

GILLIE: Girls are smarter than boys, you know.
WILLIE: I never knew that.
GILLIE: See what I mean?

SIMON: Susie's really clever, you know. She has the brains for two.
SIDNEY: Then she's just the girl for you.

COLONEL BLIMP: I shot a five-metre lion when I was in Africa.
MAJOR WIMP: That was some lyin'.

JAN: My boyfriend thinks I look like an Italian dish.
DAN: He's right.
JAN: Which one? Sophia Loren?
DAN: No, spaghetti bolognese.

HOTEL MANAGER: I hope you enjoyed your stay, sir.
GUEST: I did. But I'm sorry to be leaving your hotel so soon after practically buying it.

MIKE: My doctor told me to exercise with a dumb-bell.
SPIKE: So?
MIKE: So come to the gym with me then.

TED: Do you think I'm a fool?
NED: No. But what's my opinion against that of thousands of others?

Three ladies were standing up on a train, and one very fat lady was sitting down. She turned to the man sitting next to her and said, 'If you were a gentleman, you'd stand up and let one of those ladies sit down.'

'And if you were a lady,' he replied, 'you'd stand up and let all three of them sit down.'

Henry thought he was very funny and went around looking for new people to tell his jokes to. But the trouble was that his jokes were truly dreadful.

One day he managed to corner a man on a train for a whole hour, and told him all his jokes.

At last, as the man was about to get off, he asked Henry, 'Do you make up all your own jokes?'

'Yes,' replied Henry. 'Out of my head.'

'You must be,' said the man as he climbed down from the train.

MRS BASSINET: My new baby is the image of me.
MRS PERAMBULATOR: Never mind, as long as it's healthy.

VISITOR: Have you told your little girl to stop imitating me?
MOTHER: Yes, I told her to stop playing the fool.

GEORGINA: What happened to that dumb blonde Johnny used to go out with?
GLORIA: I dyed my hair.

TERRY: Roger's very dependable.
GERRY: Yes. You can always depend on him to do the wrong thing.

BARBER: Your hair is getting grey, sir.
CUSTOMER: I'm not surprised, with the time I've been sitting here waiting.

SALLY: Bill keeps telling me he's going to marry the most beautiful girl in the world.
SUSIE: What a shame! And after you've been engaged to him all these years!

'His ears are so big he looks like a car with its doors open.'

'I wouldn't say he was stupid, but when he went to a mind-reader he got his money back.'

How do you spot the idiot in the car wash?
He's the one on the motorbike.

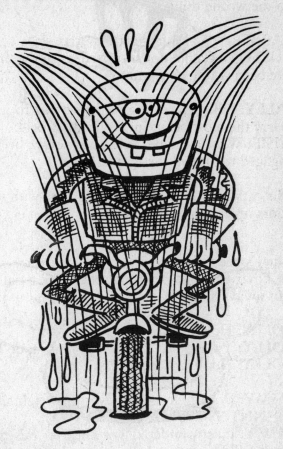

'What does your brain want to be when it grows up?'

'That dress fits you like a glove. It's a shame it doesn't fit you like a dress.'

What sort of children do florists have?
Blooming idiots!

'Mary's been planning a runaway marriage with her boyfriend, but every time they pick a date he runs away.'

HOLLY: How old are you?
DOLLY: Twenty-six. But I don't look it, do I?
HOLLY: No, but you used to.

JIMMY: Does your mother ever lift weights?
JOHNNY: No. Why?
JIMMY: I just wondered how she ever raised a dumb-bell like you.

JOHN: Since I heard that fish is good for the brain I've eaten it all the time.
DON: Another theory bites the dust!

TIM: How do you keep an idiot in suspense?
JIM: I don't know.
TIM: Tell you next week.

MRS SNOOTY: I always use lemon juice for my complexion.
MRS BOOTY: I expect that's why you look so sour.

'He thinks everyone worships the ground he crawled out of.'

'That singer's success has gone to his head.'
'Well, it certainly hasn't gone to his voice.'

MARIA: Our dog is just like one of the family.
TERESA: Oh really? Your brother?

MOTHER: Be careful with your cooking, Julie, most accidents happen in the kitchen, you know.
JULIE: Yes. I have to eat them.

EDDIE: We bumped into some old friends yesterday.
FREDDIE: Was your Dad driving again?

MR HUMPTY: How old is your wife?
MR DUMPTY: Approaching forty.
MR HUMPTY: From which direction?

'Did you hear about the idiot motorist who couldn't find the M25?'
'He went up and down the M1 twenty-five times.'

WAYNE: My new girlfriend has beautiful red hair all down her back.
JAYNE: Pity it's not on her head.

Raspberries and Cream

'Should you eat raspberries with your fingers?'
'No, fingers should be eaten separately.'
TEACHER: Order, children, order!
CHEEKY CHARLIE: Raspberries and cream, please.

Knock, knock.
Who's there?
Alma.
Alma who?
Alma raspberries have gone.

JANET: I don't like this raspberry shortcake.
MUM: I've been making raspberry shortcake since before you were born.
JANET: Why did you have to save some for me?

What do you call a boy who's eaten six bowls of raspberries?
Berry greedy.

What do you call a boy who's eaten sixty bowls of raspberries?
Berry ill.

What do you get if you cross a tonne of raspberries with a hundred cars?
Traffic jam.

Knock, knock.
Who's there?
Ben.
Ben who?
Ben making raspberry ice-cream.

Knock, knock.
Who's there?
Celeste.
Celeste who?
Celeste time I give you a bowl of raspberries.

What's red and white and travels faster than sound?
A bowl of raspberries on Concorde.

MARJORIE: Are slugs nice to eat, Mum?
MUM: Don't be disgusting. Eat your dinner.

MUM (LATER): What was that you were saying about slugs?
MARJORIE: You had one in your raspberries but it's gone now.

'Waiter, there aren't any raspberries in this raspberry tart!'
'There aren't any shepherds in the shepherds' pie, either.'

Why do people serve raspberries in round bowls?
Because they give you a lovely round feeling in your stomach.

NEWSPAPER ANNOUNCEMENT: The hot weather has caused ice-cream salesmen to order huge socks.

If you get honey from a bee, what do you get from a wasp?
Waspberry jam.

LITTLE BOY: Will you give me some money for a raspberry lolly?
MAN: No thanks, I don't like raspberry lollies.

Knock, knock.
Who's there?
Arthur.
Arthur who?
Arthur any raspberries left?

'Waiter, this raspberry fool tastes funny!'
'Then why aren't you laughing, sir?'

A greedy young maiden called Emma
Was seized with an internal tremor.
She'd scoffed lots of berries,
Bananas and cherries –
Now she's in an awful dilemma.

What's the difference between a raspberry and a cockroach?
Have you ever tried eating cockroach ice-cream?

A not very bright man ran several yards down the road after a fire engine. When he got too out of breath to run any further, he called out, 'OK, keep your rotten ice-cream.'

Knock, knock.
Who's there?
Emma.
Emma who?
Emma pig when it comes to raspberries.

JIM: Yesterday we had repeating pudding.
KIM: What's repeating pudding?
JIM: Raspberry boo-meringue.

'Waiter, there's a film on my raspberries and cream.'
'Have you seen it before, sir?'

What do you get if you cross a pound of raspberries with an elephant?
A jar of jam that never forgets.

Knock, knock.
Who's there?
Cynthia.
Cynthia who?
Cynthia been away I've eaten all your raspberries.

Knock, knock.
Who's there?
Norma Lee.
Norma Lee who?
Norma Lee I don't like raspberries, but . . .

Knock, knock.
Who's there?
Cyril.
Cyril who?
Cyril pleasure to eat raspberries and cream.

CUSTOMER: What kind of ice-cream do you have?
WAITER, CROAKING: Raspberry, strawberry and vanilla.
CUSTOMER, SYMPATHETIC: Do you have laryngitis?
WAITER: No, just raspberry, strawberry and vanilla.

'Doctor, Doctor, I feel like a raspberry lolly.'
'So do I, let's go out and buy some.'

Knock, knock.
Who's there?
Jimmy.
Jimmy who?
Jimmy a little bit of your ice-cream, please.

A tramp called at a big house and asked for food.
   'Didn't I give you a slice of my raspberry cake last week?' asked the lady at the door.
   'Yes, but I'm better now,' replied the tramp.

'Waiter, why is my raspberry tart all squashed?'
'Well, you did ask me to step on it, sir.'

MAN IN THEATRE: I think you're sitting in my seat.
OTHER MAN IN THEATRE: Can you prove it?
FIRST MAN: Yes, I left a slice of raspberry tart on it.

Knock, knock.
Who's there?
Stu.
Stu who?
Stu late to eat raspberries.

Knock, knock.
Who's there?
Dozen.
Dozen who?
Dozen anyone want this last bowl of raspberries?

Knock, knock.
Who's there?
Maida.
Maida who?
Maida raspberry cake 'cos I knew you were coming.

Knock, knock.
Who's there?
Fred.
Fred who?
Fred I've eaten all your raspberries.

There once was a young man named Sid
Who ate twenty tarts for a quid.
When asked, 'Are you faint?'
He replied, 'No, I ain't,
But I don't feel as well as I did.'

FIRST GARDENER: What do you put on your raspberries?
SECOND GARDENER: Cow manure.
FIRST GARDENER: Really? I put cream on mine.

'Waiter, there's a fly in my raspberry ice-cream.'
'That'll be 50p extra, sir.'

Knock, knock.
Who's there?
Hannah.
Hannah who?
Hannah nother bowl of raspberries and cream, please.

'Waiter, there's a dead fly in my raspberry water ice!'
'Yes, sir, it's the cold that kills them.'

BELINDA: I eaten six raspberry tarts.
MUM: Ate, Belinda, ate.
BELINDA: It may have been eight, all I know is I eaten an awful lot.

'Waiter, is there raspberry trifle on the menu?'
'There was, sir, but I wiped it off.'

Knock, knock.
Who's there?
Harvey.
Harvey who?
Harvey gonna eat raspberries for ever?